DAN'S

Written by Jillian Powell
Illustrated by Frances Castle

Dan had a den.

Rav and Sam wanted to come in.

"No, you can't," said Dan.
"It is my den."

Dan hid in his den by himself.
Rav and Sam left to have a picnic.

They had some soft plums. Yum!
Next they had some milk. Gulp!

Dan sulked. He felt sad.
He did not want to be by himself.

"Can I come to the picnic?"
said Dan.

“Yes, if we can come into the den!” said Rav and Sam.